Incident & Crisis Management - removing the mystery

Guidance for large & small businesses

© HS Books

Material in this book, including text and images, is protected by copyright. It may not be copied, reproduced, republished, downloaded, posted, broadcast or transmitted in any way except for your own personal, non-commercial use. Prior written consent of the copyright holder must be obtained for any other use of material.

Disclaimer Notice

The information contained in this book is general guidance only. Nothing in this book is or purports to be advice. If you need advice you should seek personal professional advice based on your own circumstances.

HS Books and Harry Scott have tried to ensure that the information in this book is accurate. However HS Books and Harry Scott will not accept liability for any injury, loss or damage arising as a consequence of any action(s) taken following the reading of this book, or any use of, or the inability to use, any information contained within the book.

First published November 26th, 2013
Revised 6th August 2014
2nd Revision 8th January 2015

Other books by the same author.

The Radio Officer's War - Ships, Storms & Submarines.
(The story of a young Merchant Navy radio officer in action during World War 2, at the Narvik landings in Norway, and on the North Atlantic, told through his letters and journals.)

Berwick-upon-Tweed – for King and Country.
(How a typical British coastal town contributed to the fight against Germany and her allies during The Great War, including stories from her fighting men at the Front.)

Forgotten Poems and Sonnets from 'The Great War' (An anthology of poems and sonnets from World War 1.)
(A collection of forgotten poems and sonnets written by men fighting during 'The Great War', their relatives, friends, and others.)

All available from Amazon books.

Acknowledgements

Sincere thanks go to the following colleagues for reviewing the content of this book and providing much constructive feedback:-

Douglas Borthwick, Co-ordinator (Lothian & Borders), East of Scotland Regional Resilience Partnership, Police Scotland, Edinburgh.

Jonathan Hemus, Managing Director, Insignia Communications, Sutton Coldfield, West Midlands.

Dennis LaDucer, Assistant Sheriff (Operations) (Retired), Orange County Sheriff-Coroner Department, California, USA.

Watson McAteer, FSyI, Head of Regions, Corporate Security Services at Royal Bank of Scotland.

Gerry Neish, Chief Inspector (Retired), Events & Contingency Planning Section, Lothian and Borders Police, Edinburgh.

Doctor Brian Plastow, Lead Inspector, Her Majesty's Inspectorate of Constabulary for Scotland.

Steve Sansom, Commander (Retired), Jackson, Mississippi Police Department

Evelyn Watson, Principle Teacher of Social Studies, Scottish Borders Council Department of Education.

Contents.   **Page.**

About the Author	6
Introduction.	8
What can businesses do to prepare?	9
What is 'Command & Control', and where does it fit into routine business operations?	9
What are common reactions to emergencies and why does incident management fail**?**	12
Are good leaders born or made? What are the symptoms and consequences of poor leadership?	13
How can I prepare before taking part in an incident management meeting, and what tools can I use?	15
How should an incident management meeting be conducted?	19
How should the Chair of an incident management team lead the group?	20

- Establishing the rules for the conduct of meetings.
- What are the other issues/actions the Chair needs to consider or implement?
- Table - Use of authority by the leader.

What support does an incident management meeting require?	24

- Deputy Chair.
- Incident Room Manager.
- Secretary to incident management team.
- Recording and logging team.
- Equipment and facilities.
- How long should I be expected to work as the member of an incident management team?

How should businesses respond to the media during an incident?	29
How should I communicate with employees, customers, and others?	31
What methods can I use to exercise my business continuity and incident management plans?	32
Incident review and debriefing.	33
Should I invest in a computerised business continuity/incident management system?	34
Conclusion.	35
Appendices.	36 - 44

Appendix 'A' – Incident management team policy decision log.
Appendix 'B' – Model agenda for first meeting of incident management team.
Appendix 'C' – Using focus boards.
Appendix 'D' – Appointment of a briefing officer and preparation of situation reports.
Appendix 'E' – Message/action record form – incoming & outgoing calls and messages.
Appendix 'F' – Debriefing the incident.
Appendix 'G' – Action plan following a live event or emergency exercise.

References.	45

About the Author

Harry Scott enjoyed a Police career spanning over 30 years during which time he was the police incident officer during many emergency situations, as well as being in charge of major sporting and public events.

In 2004 he was appointed National Emergencies Planning Officer for the Scottish Government Health Department where he chaired groups responding to emergencies at national level, e.g. industrial disputes involving the distribution of fuel to the NHS, and planning large scale national exercises e.g. Scotland's response to pandemic influenza, and the NHS response to incidents involving terrorism. His last appointment was as a Business Continuity Manager at Royal Bank of Scotland, managing a team of 10 business continuity consultants, providing support and guidance to around 180 varied business units throughout the RBS Group.

Harry was a full Member of the Business Continuity Institute for many years, and in 2002 gained a Master of Science Degree in Risk, Crisis and Disaster Management. He has lectured at the Scottish Police College, the University of Edinburgh Medical School, the University of Paisley, and Borders College. He has also presented at several conferences and workshops dealing with emergency preparedness and business continuity planning, and has published articles on the BCI and Continuity Central web sites:-

'The Importance of Conducting Effective Crisis Meetings' - BCI Workshop January 2009.
'In the Hot Seat – Chairing a Crisis Management Meeting' – Continuity Central May 2009.
'A Plan is not a Plan until it is Exercised and Validated' - BCI Workshop August 2008.

Past Membership & Chairing of Committees:-

1. Chair of NHS Scotland Emergency Planning Officers' Forum (now NHSScotland Resilience Forum), providing emergency preparedness advice to the Scottish Government Health Department and NHS Scotland.

2. Chair of NHS Scotland Critical National Infrastructure Group, providing protective security & counter terrorism advice to the Scottish Government Health Department and NHS Scotland.

3. Member of CONTEST (Counter Terrorism) Scotland Board, providing protective security and counter terrorism advice to Scottish Government Ministers.

4. Member of Resilience Advisory Board for Scotland (RABS), providing strategic contingency planning advice to Scottish Government Ministers.

5. Member of RABS Exercising & Training Group, chaired by the Scottish Resilience Development Service (ScoRDS), formulating national strategy for major emergency exercising and training in Scotland.

6. Member of Centre for Protection of National Infrastructure (CPNI) Health Sector Working Group, providing protective security & counter terrorism advice to the NHS in the UK and N. Ireland.

7. Member of the Scottish Government Critical National Infrastructure (CNI) Group, tasked with improving the resilience & protective security of critical national infrastructure sites located in Scotland.

Introduction

The term *'incident'* is defined in the Cambridge Dictionary as *"an event that is either unpleasant or unusual"*. The term *'crisis'* is defined as *"an extremely difficult or dangerous point in a situation"*, or *"a sudden loss of confidence"*.

Having business continuity arrangements in place will assist businesses to survive the effect of incidents which have the potential to cause severe disruption, or worse, to their business operations. Small and medium sized businesses may find putting these arrangements in place a challenge, working as they do in a very competitive market place, in an ever changing environment, and with a limited number of staff, but they should try in order to improve the odds of surviving an incident which might cause major damage to the business. Remember that a disaster for one business may well be an opportunity for another to take its place!

No matter how well business continuity plans are written or put together there must be a strong management structure in place for kicking them into action when required, otherwise they will be of little use. Much of the literature on business continuity planning will allude to this, but there is not much guidance on how an incident management team should function.

The simpler you can keep any incident management system the better. This book aims to give senior managers and employees uncomplicated, no-jargon guidance from a practitioner's point of view, on how to put in place a strong and effective structure for managing disruptive incidents.

The information provided in this book is general guidance. It needs to be adapted to suit individual businesses which should use the information to develop their own detailed emergency response procedures. Businesses should, where appropriate, seek qualified professional advice.

What can businesses do to prepare?

Although anything can happen, the majority of emergencies, major or minor, will occur through one of the following causes:-

1. Fire.
2. Flooding and severe weather.
3. Denial of access to premises.
4. Failure of utilities - electric, gas or water.
5. Collapse of a key supplier.
6. Sudden loss of key or specialist staff.
7. Sudden enforcement action by an industry regulator, e.g. Environment Agency, Vehicle and Operator Services Agency, Financial Services Authority etc. etc.

Although getting business continuity and incident management arrangements in place may be challenging, there are uncomplicated steps which can be taken to enable a structured response to the occurrence of a disruptive incident. There are many useful guidance documents produced by the Business Continuity Institute, the Federation of Small Businesses, and the UK Government Cabinet Office, which will allow businesses and organisations to tailor their business continuity arrangements to their own particular needs.

What is 'Command & Control' and where does it fit into routine business operations?

During the 1980s a widespread series of inner city riots occurred in the UK. Policing arrangements to deal with these riots were found to be inadequate, and led to the one and only time when UK mainland police in Liverpool used tear gas against rioters. In the aftermath of these riots the police service developed a three-tiered, 'Command and Control' structure which introduced strategic, tactical and operational levels of management, commonly known as 'Gold', 'Silver' and 'Bronze' to respond to major emergencies and large scale public events.

Strategic (Gold) managers or commanders set the strategy for tackling a task. Tactical (Silver) managers or commanders implement the policy decided at strategic level and allocate tasks and deploy personnel and resources to achieve the task. Operational (Bronze) managers or commanders manage the resources on the ground, and lead the individuals carrying out the tasks.

A command and control structure exists in most businesses. A board of directors will set the strategy for the business. Senior managers will decide the tactics and will direct and co-ordinate the deployment of staff and resources to achieve that strategy. Middle or junior managers will deal with the day to day operations involved in running the business efficiently. **There must be clear and regular communication between each level of management, especially assessments from operational managers to those at the higher levels.**

At each level of the management structure there will be problems to be dealt with, options to be considered, and solutions to be put in place. Sometimes the dynamics in the day to day management of the business will be similar to those during a sudden emergency, e.g. completion of a major money earning contract within strict time limits, processing a rush order for an important client, or sudden failure of a key supplier.

Businesses come in all shapes and sizes. Whilst some may be able to separate clearly the three levels of management, there will be many more that can't because of their limited size. For example in a small company employing about 10 staff or less, the business owner or a small group of managers and supervisors, may be responsible for setting the strategy for the business as well as being responsible for the day to day functions at tactical and operational level.

Managing an incident in such circumstances will demand clarity of thinking, and may place great strain on the personnel concerned. However having clear management structures, with clearly defined roles and responsibilities, will aid significantly the management response to most situations.

The command and control structure can be initiated at any of the levels described. It may be initiated at operational level by a fire or flooding at a building, or at tactical level by a sudden computer failure that affects several services or departments across a business. It may be initiated at strategic level in the case of some catastrophic event, or in preparation for a foreseen emergency such as pandemic influenza, or large scale public events where severe disruption might be expected.

In a great many cases incidents will be successfully resolved at operational or tactical level, as in the conduct of normal day to day business. However there will be instances where escalation to strategic level is required and there needs to be clear guidance on how the business achieves this.

Basic Model of Command and Control

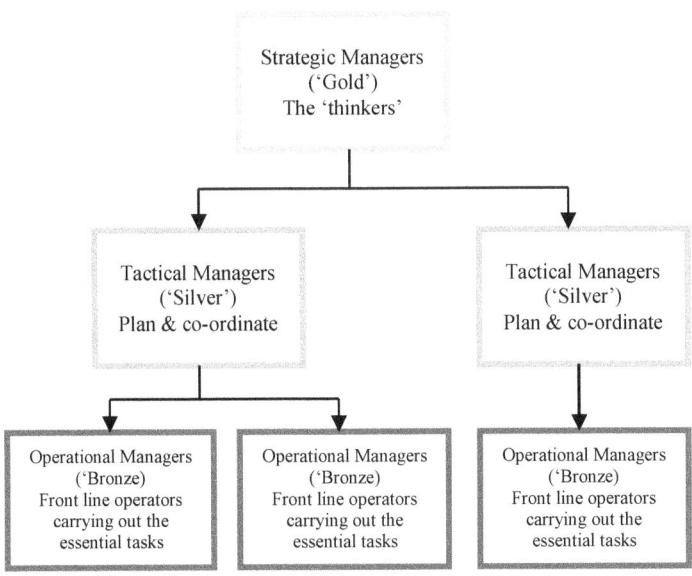

What are common reactions to emergencies and why does incident management fail?

The sudden onset of a major emergency can trigger various unwelcome reactions in different people. It can result in:-

1. Absolute panic.
2. The 'headless chicken' syndrome where everyone appears to be busy, but there is no clear direction and not a lot is being achieved.
3. The 'bull at a gate' syndrome, where certain individuals will steam ahead without giving much thought to the consequences of what they are doing, or adopting a threatening style of management to disguise their own failings.
4. The 'Blackadder' syndrome, where to quote from General Sir Anthony Melchett, *"A pig headed unwillingness to look facts in the face will see us through"*. (BBC TV 'Blackadder Goes Forth, 1989).

In my previous service with the Police, the National Health Service, and Government I have witnessed all four. Panic in a leader is a most infectious disease and will spread quickly to others if not checked. I have also witnessed senior personnel vanish from the scene – no one could find them, go ill with the stress, and one who had the honesty to tell me that they could not cope with the situation. Finding the right people for the job is essential.

If incident management fails it is generally as a result of a combination of factors such as not having an understanding of the events which have taken place and the possible consequences for the business, poor leadership and decision-making ability, stress, and using the wrong or unfamiliar structures or procedures.

As soon as the words 'emergency', 'crisis', or 'incident' are used, what I term as a 'red mist' occasionally comes down over the eyes of some, and they may be struck by feelings of dread and/or apprehension at the thought of dealing with the unknown. These are natural feelings and even the best leaders will admit to them.

There is no shame in admitting to having those feelings and sharing them with colleagues, who will possibly be feeling the same, is likely to bring a team closer together. Such feelings may be experienced during the normal day to day running of the business e.g. initiating a new business process which has not been tried before, and which is untested. During the 'Battle of The Atlantic' even Winston Churchill admitted that, *"The only thing that ever really frightened me during the war was the U-boat peril. I was even more anxious about this battle than I had been about the glorious air fight called the Battle of Britain."*

Are good leaders born or made? What are the symptoms and consequences of poor leadership?

The answer to the first question is, probably a bit of both. Most people who aspire to management want to lead, so the desire must be there. Not all will be 'born' to it, but they can be trained. Look at your own organisation and others. The armed forces, civilian services, and industry, all have the ability to develop excellent leaders through rigorous training. It's a fair bet that not all of them were 'born' to it.

Managing dynamic situations where there may be much to lose is stressful. Not everyone is naturally up to the challenge, and leaders need to have the ability to analyse huge amounts of information in less than ideal circumstances. This is true, not only during an emergency, but perhaps where complicated contracts are being negotiated within a short timescale, or a sudden surge in production is required, which means employing practices outwith the norm. Training is required, among other things, in the art of chairing meetings, managing diverse groups, being able to assess what is happening, and what the likely outcome for the business will be.

Poor leadership comes in many forms, and I have experienced most. Several years ago I was in charge of the Police Firearms Support Unit during an anti-terrorist exercise at a major international airport. I found it very difficult dealing with the Police Incident Commander who used a very threatening manner, and who ran about most of the time shouting and swearing at his subordinates. This caused nervousness in them in case they caught the brunt of his disapproval. It curtailed initiative and resulted in much inertia in the management of the incident.

Thankfully the Police Incident Commander who relieved him was quite different. He was calm, cool and collected, and had briefed himself well. More importantly he gathered his senior officers around him and encouraged them to come to him with suggestions for resolving the incident. Personnel gained in confidence, and provided the Incident Commander with sound advice, which brought the incident to a successful conclusion. They were also not afraid to bring him bad news, unlike to his predecessor, who had a habit of 'shooting the messenger'.

Sadly I like John Wayne films, but there are a couple of scenes in the film, *'She Wore a Yellow Ribbon'* where he says, *"Never apologise, it's a sign of weakness."* I'm of the opinion it's a sign of stupidity and found mainly in leaders who bluster, or who use a threatening manner towards their subordinates to mask their own insecurity. People are not stupid and they will be well aware of when you make a mistake, and whether you are up to the task. Don't try and hide mistakes. Admit them, apologise for them if necessary, and then move on. Your colleagues will empathise and you will earn greater respect by showing that you are indeed human. In a fast moving environment where decisions have to be made based on information which is incomplete, or even wrong, mistakes **will** be made.

How can I prepare before taking part in an incident management meeting, and what tools can I use?

Being part of an incident management team will seldom be easy, and there will be many unknowns. You may have to work with information which is incomplete, misleading, or even wrong, but by being as prepared as you can you will be able to contribute meaningfully to the business of the team and enable it to make clear decisions as quickly as possible

Find out as much as you can beforehand, and be ready to discuss the following:-

1. What has happened?
2. What does the incident mean for your area of responsibility?
3. What are the short and medium term implications for your area?
4. What options are available to you to mitigate the effects of the incident?
5. What course of remedial action might you recommend to the Chair?
6. What is the impact on other areas that are either dependent on you, or who you are dependent upon?
7. Who at that meeting might be able to assist you, and who might you assist?

You may not be able to achieve all that listed above, but even by achieving some of the points you may be able to structure your thinking before the meeting convenes.

At the first meeting introduce yourself and explain clearly your role and responsibilities. The Chair of the group will need to establish if the right people are there. It is essential that you are empowered to make decisions on behalf of your department without referral to higher authority, and you will need to establish that before you go. If you are not, you are of limited use and you should try for someone with the required level of authority to attend in your place. During the meeting you should:-

1. Note the names of the members and the departments or agencies they represent so that you can identify individuals that may be able to assist you, or who you might be able to assist.
2. Ensure you are clear about the strategy set for the incident management team and ensure that you follow it as best you can.
3. Be clear about any actions placed on you by the Chair or requests from others around the table. A good Chair and their Deputy will monitor the progress of these actions and if not completed will want to know why.
4. Make sure that you keep a comprehensive note of what is discussed at the meeting, especially issues directly related to you. This will enable you to clear up any ambiguities if what is in the subsequent minute of the meeting does not truly reflect what you said or what you meant to say.
5. Declare any potential conflicts of interest, e.g. conflicting interests or priorities relating to the need for limited resources etc.
6. When speaking use plain language and avoid using technical jargon and abbreviations that others might not understand.
7. Take care and be clear so that what you say cannot be construed as having another meaning.

There are tools which can assist in alleviating some of the apprehension when you are tasked with either initiating an incident management plan, or requested to join an incident management team. Using an aide memoir will help you prepare for incident management meetings and two examples are shown in the following pages.

Example of an aide memoir to assist in noting essential details when informed that an incident has occurred – this can be tailored or adapted to suit the individual business concerned.

Gathering the information below will aid you in assessing what has happened and the possible consequences for the business. It will also assist in structuring your thinking before any meeting.

INCIDENT DETAILS (this should be tailored to suit your own business structure)	NOTES:-
1. Who is telling you? Note date & time. 2. What has happened? 3. When did it happen? 4. Where did it happen? 5. Which department(s) is involved? 6. What are the short and medium term issues for the business? 7. Are the emergency services involved? 8. If the emergency services are involved have they declared a major incident?	
IMMEDIATE ACTIONS (this should be tailored to suit your own business structure)	
1. Begin a log of events. 2. Contact a member of the Incident Management Team. 3. Discuss whether the Incident Management Team needs to be convened. 4. If so find suitable place for a meeting of the Incident Management Team	
WHO NEEDS TO BE INFORMED (this should be tailored to suit your own business structure)	
1. IT staff? 2. HR staff? 3. Finance? 4. Key suppliers to stop deliveries? 5. Transport Section? 6. Security? 7. Facilities?	

This flow chart, used, in conjunction with the aide-memoire, is to provide guidance to personnel responsible for initiating contingency plans. It should be tailored to the needs of your own business, and contact information can be entered into the boxes as required.

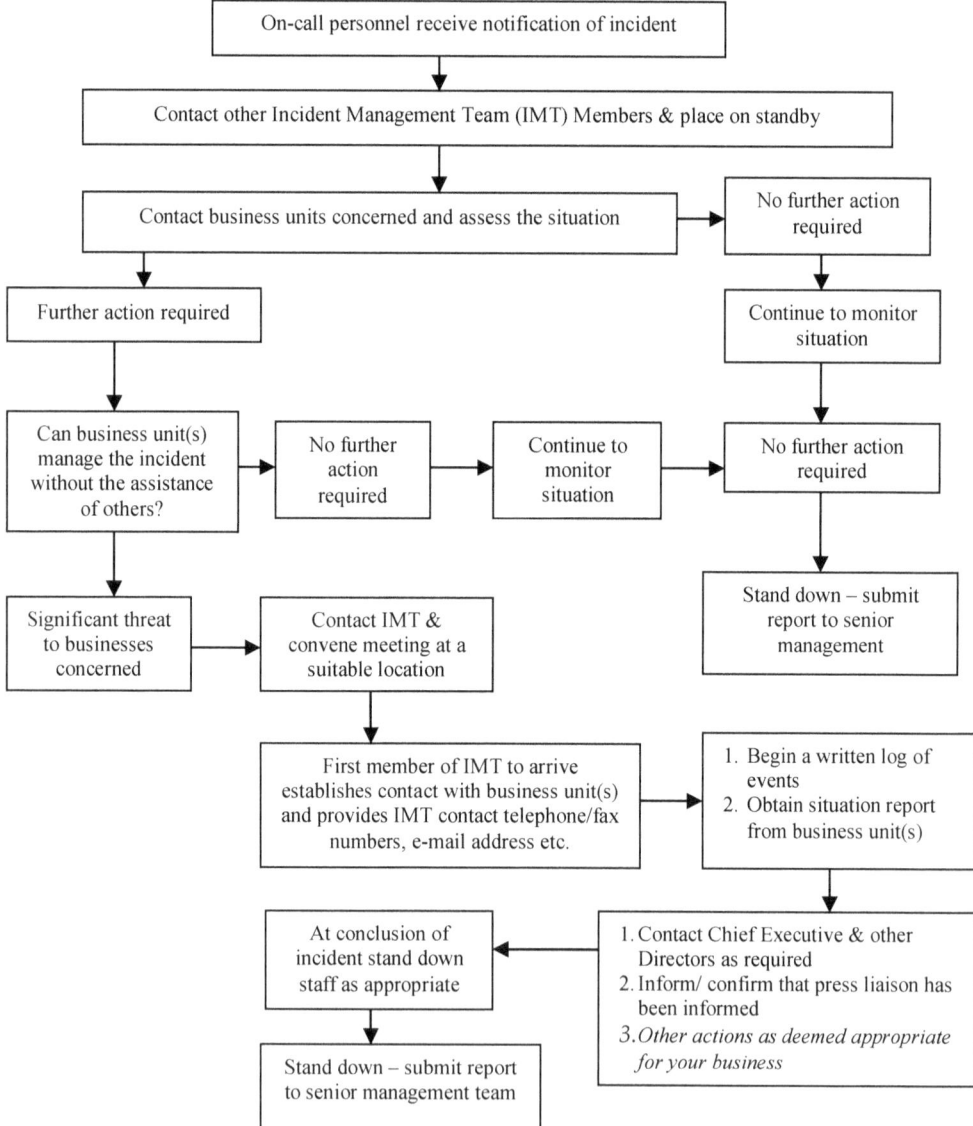

How should an incident management meeting be conducted?

Incident management meetings should be conducted in a manner which is as near to your normal business practice as possible as there is little point in introducing to you and your staff, unfamiliar methods which will be little used. Irrespective of any training, people will forget as these methods will not be part of everyday working practice (***The objective is for business continuity planning to become just a normal part of the way that the organisation operates, so that unless there are valid reasons against it, the incident response structure should mirror the organisation's existing management structure***) *(BCI Good Practice Guidelines, 2013)*.

Although the dynamics may be different and demand that decisions are made quickly, there will be similarities with normal business meetings in that you will be discussing, among the other issues, the efficient use of time, people, and resources.

Incident management meetings should be time limited to no more than 25-30 minutes after which the attendees should leave to carry out any tasks allocated to them, or talk to other colleagues who can assist them in dealing with the incident. An incident management meeting should not become a forum for protracted debate, but a forum for putting forward options and recommendations for corrective action, and deciding what to do. Incident management team members have to be very clear and focussed in their thinking and brief and to the point.

Where problems are identified efforts should be made to solve them outwith the meeting, either by your own efforts, or by talking to colleagues who can assist. Problems, if at all possible, should not be left to be discussed at the meeting. This will enable members to come to the table highlighting issues which have been identified and recommending a course of remedial action to the Chair of the incident management team.

Where individuals disagree with what is in the minute of the meeting they should endeavour, where possible, to rectify or agree some compromise with the Chair of the meeting, or other individual(s) concerned before the next meeting is convened.

That will prevent the incident management team meeting being bogged down by argument, or protracted debate.

How should the Chair of an incident management team lead the group?

The role of the incident management team Chair is to provide leadership, and direct and co-ordinate incident management team meetings. The Chair should be responsible for ensuring that the incident management team functions effectively and provides the necessary advice, guidance or instruction, to support the effective management of the incident.

It is essential for the Chair to establish that the right people are at the incident management team meeting and that they are empowered to make decisions on behalf of their organisation or department. If they are not they are of limited value and steps should be taken to secure the attendance of some person with the required level of authority.

Meetings may sometimes be conducted by telephone or video link. The Chair, or Secretary to the team, when all the people required have joined the meeting, should repeat the name of each individual and the department or agency they represent for the benefit of all the members, as it is unlikely that all will join the link at the same time.

Establishing the rules for the conduct of meetings:-

1. Members must recognise the authority and co-ordinating role of the Chair of the team.
2. Recognise the role of the team, *as a team,* working together to resolve a difficult situation.
3. Members of the team to have clarity about their role and consult the Chair if in any doubt.
4. Only key members will be invited to attend meetings, with others being requested to attend as required.
5. Team members must attend meetings promptly at the time stated.
6. Meetings will be limited to 25-30 minutes with any follow-up action taken off-table.

7. As far as possible, options for remedial action to be formulated off-table by members and reported back to the Chair and the team.
8. All major policy decisions and the reasons for those decisions will be properly recorded (See Appendix 'A').
9. Team members will keep contributions relevant, concise, and to the point with no unnecessary debating.
10. Consensus is preferred, but where there is no unanimous agreement the Chair will have final discretion.
11. Any conflicts of interest/organisational problems are to be declared to the Chair.
12. There should be no unauthorised external communication of incident management team proceedings.
13. Members are to fully brief colleagues relieving them so that time is not wasted on repetitious briefings by the Chair or others.
14. In a teleconference members may speak only when given permission by the Chair to avoid people talking over one another.
15. In a teleconference members to keep their 'mute' button engaged unless speaking so that any background noises are kept to the minimum.

What are the other issues/actions the Chair needs to consider or implement?

1. Nominate a deputy to deputise for the Chair as and when required.
2. Make sure there is adequate administrative support in place for the team (this should not be underestimated).
3. If possible a model agenda for meetings should be provided (see Appendix 'B').
4. Agree who will link with any sub-groups e.g. media or technical.
5. Establish the strategy for the team and ensure it is followed, e.g. welfare of people, protection of property, reputation etc.
6. Ensure that an incident management team focus board is initiated and maintained (see Appendix 'C').

7. Keep the team's objectives achievable and don't try and do too much (see Appendix 'C').
8. Appoint a briefing officer and ensure that situation reports are prepared and distributed at regular intervals for the information of senior management and others engaged in managing the incident (see Appendix 'D').
9. Think ahead and consider the future implications of any decisions made or actions contemplated.
10. Note lessons as incident progresses for debriefing and subsequent evaluation.
11. Decisions should be made on the best possible information available and not delayed unduly until the ideal information becomes available.
12. Team meetings should have accurate minutes taken with rapid turnaround and distribution.
13. Meetings may have to be co-ordinated with others e.g. the emergency services, local authority, or specialist meetings within the business, to enable the Chair or another team member to attend those meetings.
14. Arrange a phased handover during prolonged incidents i.e. relief of members staggered so that all the thinking of the group does not leave the table at the same time.
15. Do not be afraid to have a change of mind, **but** not too often as it could be perceived as being indecisive.

The Chair of an incident management team has to adopt the leadership style that is most appropriate to the situation being dealt with, and the composition of the team being led.

That style could vary from autocratic where the team is fairly inexperienced or unsure about the process to be followed, through to a more consensual approach, when the team is very experienced at managing incidents, or where its knowledge of the business process is greater than the Chair's. This is illustrated in the table on the following page.

Use of authority by the leader

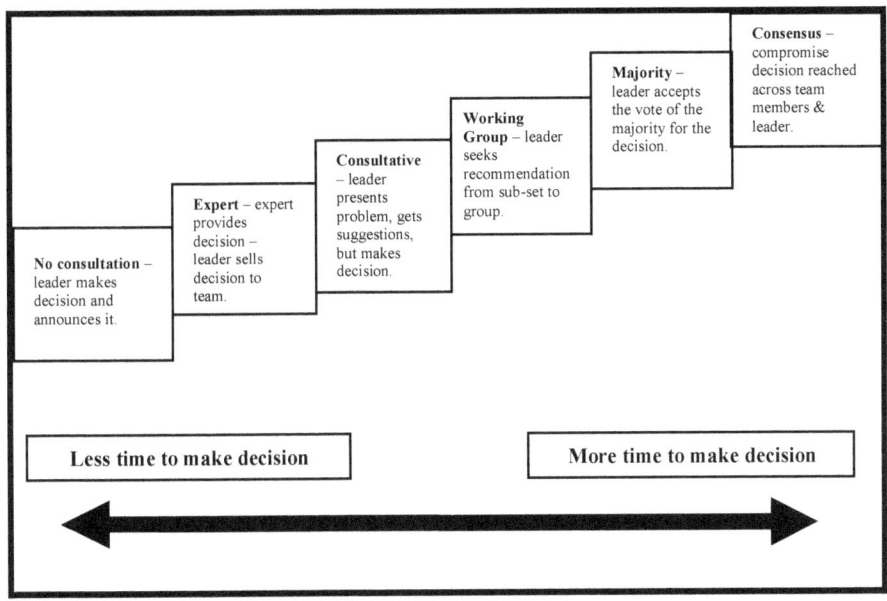

What support does an incident management meeting require?

Not only do incident management team meetings need to be well conducted, they also need to be well supported. In addition to the Chair other appointments must be made:-

1. Deputy Chair
2. Incident Room Manager
3. Secretary
4. Recording and logging team

Large businesses may be able to predetermine these appointments and earmark specially trained individuals, but smaller businesses may have to work with the personnel available and the functions performed by fewer people. Nonetheless, as long as the roles of each appointment are clearly assigned, they may be manageable, even if one individual has to perform more than one.

What are the duties of the Deputy Chair?

The Deputy should be a strong character who is not afraid to challenge others who are not performing effectively. The role includes:-

1. Supporting the Chair of the incident management team as required.
2. Ensuring that the incident management team policy decision log is established and that all major decisions are recorded, including the reasons for those decisions.
3. Noting the actions placed on others and summing them up at the end of the meeting.
4. If necessary asking individuals concerned if they fully understand what is required of them.
5. In between meetings if actions are urgent, follow up with the individuals concerned as to the progress being made, and any perceived delays.
6. Keep the Chair of team updated on progress of actions.
7. Identify any key issues for inclusion in advice or for discussion at team meetings.
8. Ensure that the incident management team focus board is updated as required.

What are the duties of the Incident Room Manager?

1. Responsible for ensuring that the incident management team room is set-up according to the plan.
2. Supervision of the recording and logging team.
3. Oversee the functioning of the incident management team room.
4. Ensure phones, faxes, e-mail facilities are working and establish procedure and rules for managing incoming and outgoing messages.
5. Ensure that all telephone calls, messages, enquiries and actions are logged.
6. Maintain a list of all staff present and the business units they represent.
7. Establish and maintain events log from time of alert onwards.
8. Ensure the maintenance of the team focus board on a whiteboard or flip chart according to the instructions of the Chair or Deputy Chair.
9. Ensure that all internal and external contact details are listed and displayed prominently in the incident management team room.
10. Set up a system for communicating significant decisions & situation reports to other members of the team – information centre or notice board.
11. Ensure the incident management team has adequate administrative support.
12. Arrange provision of food and drink.
13. Maintain a personal log.

What are the duties of the Secretary to the incident management team?

1. Providing a dedicated minute taking service to the incident management team Chair
2. Distributing minutes to team members when agreed by Chair or Deputy Chair of the team.

The importance of this task should not be underestimated. Where possible it should be performed by a shorthand typist who can quickly type up the minutes for distribution at the end of the meeting. In larger businesses there may be two secretaries working in relay, so that minutes are typed as the meeting progresses, and distributed with the minimum of delay after being cleared by the Chair.

It is important that minutes of meetings are distributed as quickly as possible after the meeting so that those attending have an opportunity to study them and either agree or challenge them, especially where they have dissented on some point. **For that reason the minute taker should not, where possible, be allocated other tasks.**

If minutes are recorded on a computer as the meeting progresses, they should be printed off immediately the meeting concludes, and given to the Chair or Deputy Chair to be cleared, before being distributed.

What are the duties of the recording and logging team?

The importance of accurately recording policy decisions taken and the reasons why, and incoming and outgoing communications to the incident management team, cannot be emphasised enough, as all documentation will likely be audited and scrutinised following any incident.

The recording and logging team's duties include:-

1. Providing administrative and clerical support to the incident management team.
2. Maintaining the incident management team focus board at the direction of the Chair or Deputy Chair & preparation of situation reports.
3. Maintaining communication logs (see Appendix 'E').
4. Maintaining the information centre/briefing board & update as required.
5. Typing and photocopying.
6. Delivering messages/documents to incident management team members as required.
7. Undertaking any other specific tasks/roles as determined by the Incident Room Manager.

What equipment and facilities does an incident management meeting require?

Many large businesses, the emergency services, and many local authorities have dedicated incident management rooms specially set aside for dealing with major emergencies. These rooms will have all the necessary communication equipment, computers and stationary etc. available for immediate use. Few medium and small businesses will be able to afford similar facilities, however they may be able to manage by planning out accommodation which they use for the day to day operation of their business as an incident management room when required.

Space and facilities for the incident management team should be pre-identified if possible, and detailed instructions and sketch plans provided in advance to enable a rapid conversion and setup of the accommodation as an incident management room. To cater for the possibility of access being denied to the workplace, other premises should be identified as alternatives, e.g. local hotels, conferencing premises, or available temporary office accommodation from companies such as 'Regus' or the local authority.

The incident management team should, as a minimum, have two rooms in close proximity, or at least one large dedicated room capable of being sub-divided into a staff working area and a separate incident management team meeting area. Equipment should include:-

1. Meeting table and chairs.
2. Working desks and chairs.
3. Room dividers/screens.
4. Telephones and additional telephone points enabled with broadband and Internet connections.
5. Faxing facilities or access to them.
6. Photocopying facilities or ready access to such nearby.
7. One or more white boards, flip charts and notice boards.
8. Computers as required.

How long should I be expected to work as the member of an incident management team?

If the management of an incident is expected to last for more than 24 hours, personnel on the incident management team will require adequate rotation to minimise fatigue. **On no account should anyone be expected to function on a 24/7 basis.** As well as causing chronic fatigue, the judgment ability of that individual will deteriorate and have a detrimental effect on the effectiveness of the team and management of the incident. The Chair of the team should ensure that arrangements are in place to relieve members of the incident management team, including her/himself in circumstances where the team is obliged to convene on a 24/7 basis.

It may be appropriate to consider changing the Chair of the incident management team if the focus for advice moves on from the emergency and business recovery phases to, e.g. technical or human resource issues. Any decision to change responsibility for chairing the incident management team should be done by mutual agreement with a formal signing over procedure.

The incident management team should be stood down when it is clear that there is no continuing need to maintain such a group and in agreement with other specialist or senior management groups set up to support the incident management team function.

How should businesses respond to the media during an incident?

A designated media/press officer should be identified to provide advice to the Chair on all aspects of press/media communications, and support the incident management team, liaising as required with the press, and with the communications staff of other agencies, e.g. police, local authority, regulator etc. Managing the response to the media can become a major exercise in itself.

Training courses are run by the Cabinet Office Emergency Planning College, or private providers such as Insignia Reputation Management and Communications Consultancy, but few small and medium sized businesses may be able to afford the time to place staff on them. However there is good information to be found on the Internet, e.g. Continuity Central, on how to behave when faced by the media. A few basic rules for facing the media are listed below:-

Show empathy for people affected by the situation - Your reputation will be in much better shape if you demonstrate concern and empathy for the impact of your situation on people. Ignore this rule and the chances are you will be seen as cold, calculating and more interested in profit than people.

1. **Never say "no comment"** - In the early stages of a crisis, there are many questions you can't answer – you simply won't have the facts. But your answer must never be "no comment" - that will be translated as "you're right, I'm guilty, but for legal reasons, I can't admit that".
2. **Focus on communicating facts** - You need to quickly communicate that you are on top of the crisis, and establish the organisation as a prime provider of information about the situation. Volunteering clear and relevant facts addresses these objectives as well as filling the communication vacuum.
3. **Emphasise the actions you are taking to control the situation** - All organisations are vulnerable to crises. The ones that survive and prosper are those that are seen to manage them professionally and

effectively. Communicating the steps you are taking demonstrates you are actively managing the situation, not just reacting to events.
4. **Never speculate** - Speculation is your enemy – it leads to lurid, frequently inaccurate headlines, and a crisis spiralling out of control. An effective spokesperson rejects speculation and returns to messages focused on the facts and what the organisation is doing to manage the situation.
5. **Speak clearly and calmly** - Communicate control through your tone of voice and delivery. Not only will you provide an impression of a professional organisation handling the situation responsibly, crucially you will also ensure that your messages are received accurately.
6. **Avoid using industry jargon or company acronyms** - Using jargon or acronyms means that most people watching, reading or listening to your comments will not understand what you mean. Worse, you create an impression of an aloof organisation, out of touch with the outside world and more concerned with itself.
7. **Rehearse with a colleague before taking to the airwaves** - Making time for a fifteen minute rehearsal with a colleague before embarking on an interview gives you a chance to warm up and receive feedback on which messages resonate well – and which ones don't.
8. **Ensure your body language matches your messages** - Strong eye contact and an expression of concern – not panic! – are crucial to ensuring your words are received as you intended. Ask a viewer to describe a spokesperson and they will talk about how they "came across". Very few talk about the specific words that they said.
9. **Know and repeatedly emphasise your key messages** - A media interview is an opportunity for you to communicate important information. Plan your messages ahead of the interview and seize every opportunity to introduce them into the interview. Avoid being led by the interviewer.
(Jonathan Hemus, Insignia Reputation Management & Communications Consultancy, Continuity Central, January, 2009).

How should I communicate with employees, customers and others?

Employees, customers, and others who are considered key stakeholders in the business need to be kept informed at regular intervals, and this issue needs to be kept on the agenda of the incident management team. Being pro-active in this area of the response is essential and any business that neglects to do this puts the entire incident response at risk.

This too needs the necessary organisational structure put in place before an incident occurs. Most people will generally be tolerant and sympathetic to your situation, but what they will not tolerate is **NOT** being told what is happening. This is best demonstrated during major disruptions to travel arrangements at airports, railway stations and other major travel hubs where there is reporting by the media. The majority of complaints from the public who are interviewed are that whilst they appreciate the problems and difficulties, no one from the travel company affected is telling them anything, or very little information is filtering through.

Regular communication with customers is essential to avoid the risk of them taking their business elsewhere. Similarly with employees to avoid the risk of them looking for other employment opportunities because they do not know what progress is being made, and have lost confidence in the viability of the business.

There are many ways of communicating with employees and customers, e.g. telephone help lines, regular newsletters and company web sites, and social media. All have their place and advice on how to structure a communication strategy is available from several reputable media and communication companies which specialise in this area.

What methods can I use to exercise my business continuity and incident management plans?

No matter how well written your business continuity and incident management arrangements are, unless you exercise them they will be of little use. All your staff need to be aware of what they are and have the confidence to implement them when required. Next to actually putting business continuity and incident management arrangements in place, finding time to train staff and exercise their implementation will be most challenging for small and medium sized businesses. However it is worth the effort.

There are a few established methods of exercising emergency plans:-

1. Discussion based exercises where arrangements are discussed and responsibilities can be assigned to individuals.
2. The 'walk through' where staff may be taken to view incident management facilities and shown the equipment to be used, among other issues to be discussed or addressed.
3. Table top exercises simulating an incident and involving a realistic scenario, which can be played out in real time, or speeded up as required by the objectives of the exercise.
4. Live exercises involving the live implementation of emergency plans, e.g. with players acting in the field and actually carrying out tasks, or exercising a live shut down of processes, evacuating a building, and arranging and using transport to go to a work area recovery centre etc.

Each form of exercise has its advantages and disadvantages. Discussion and table top exercises provide more time for the players to discuss, in depth, issues which might arise, but they cannot provide the realistic feel which a live exercise can. Live exercises allow the players to experience to an extent, e.g. how a real shut down of IT facilities might feel, along with realistic interaction with other players and agencies involved in the exercise. However the dynamics of the exercise may not allow a fuller in-depth consideration of all the issues involved.

There is a natural progression from the discussion based exercise to the live exercise. Each can be used to provide staff with the knowledge and experience, and most of all the confidence to handle the response to a real emergency when it happens.

At the very least businesses should attempt to achieve getting to the table top level of exercising their business continuity and incident management arrangements. Table top exercises are easy to organise, and do not require elaborate facilities and equipment to function. Detailed guidance on training and exercising can be found on the UK Government Cabinet Office web site or Continuity Central.

Incident review and debriefing

It is essential that a formal de-brief of the incident is carried out to capture lessons identified by the incident management team members, and others involved during the course of managing the incident (see Appendix 'F' for suggested format).

Recommendations should be made on the future operation of the incident management team and initiation of business continuity arrangements. These should be circulated to all those who participated in or supported the incident management team to enable them to address any issues requiring remediation.

The issues highlighted during any de-briefing sessions should be listed in an action plan (see Appendix 'G'). That plan should list the issues to be addressed; who/what group identified it, what remedial action is required, who is responsible for addressing the issue, and a final date for completion.

The Chair of the incident management team, or some other individual chosen by executive or senior management, should be charged with ensuring that the issues are being addressed by those responsible, and submitting regular progress reports to the executive or senior management.

Should I invest in a computerised business continuity/incident management system?

Many large businesses have computerised business continuity/incident management, and message & logging systems in place, with designated staff trained to use the equipment. These systems have their merits and can improve efficiency and provide an auditable trail of messages and actions. However they are expensive to install and maintain, and their use needs to be carefully considered. No matter how simple these systems are the training implications will be considerable, especially in businesses where there may be a regular turnover of staff. Also staff trained to use the system may not always be immediately available when an incident occurs.

Computerised systems can also break down. At a large counter terrorist exercise at a brand new police command centre, I accompanied the National Health Service team taking part in the exercise. They were told that the command centre had its own computerised system for passing messages between the players in the exercise. None of the National Health Service team had been trained to use the system, but they were told that a police officer who had been trained would be assisting them. There was an IT failure and the officer was unable to log on. When the system re-started he found that he had not been trained to use the command centre system. Fortunately the National Health Service team had brought a simple paper based system which colleagues and I had designed for use by National Health Service teams. They were able to hit the ground running, and all incoming and outgoing messages were properly recorded and capable of withstanding rigorous audit. Whilst seen by some as old fashioned, paper based message/logging systems do work. They are simple to explain, unlikely to break down, and implementation can be taught to large groups of people at one short sitting.

At the conclusion of any incident there will be an enquiry of some kind, whether an internal management enquiry, one carried out by an industry regulator who has the power to impose fines or other penalty, or a judicial review which might lead to a claim for damages, or a prosecution for some breach of the law. It is vital therefore that the system of recording the actions of the incident management team, and others involved in the management of the incident, can withstand rigorous scrutiny and audit. If a computerised system is introduced it is vital that it be backed up with an alternative as a precaution against IT failure.

Conclusion

Planning for emergencies can be difficult for small and medium sized businesses in a climate where competition is keen and time and resources are in short supply. However building resilience in a business can be achieved where there is a will, and making it part of the strategy for the business. The skills and methods of conducting incident management meetings described in this book can be transferred to any meeting held in the course of conducting a business. Meetings become more focussed and the time spent on them considerably shortened. This in turn, if properly applied, should make conducting business more streamlined by encouraging people to come to business meetings having considered options and recommending what might be the correct course of action.

Planning and building a strong management structure is integral to business continuity planning, which should not be seen as a separate issue, but made part of normal business operations utilising the knowledge and expertise already existing among the staff working within the business. By building that resilience, a business will have the ability to provide an effective response, not only to emergencies and potential threats, but to sudden changes in the market or the environment in which it operates.

"Resilient organisations are forward thinking and able to adapt to changing circumstances which may have damaging effects on the organisation's ability to survive. These include such things as changes to the market in which the organisation operates, competitors, legislation, technology etc., as well as incidents that disrupt the organisation's ability to deliver its products and services."(BCI Good Practice Guidelines, 2013).

Appendix 'A'

Incident management team policy decision log

Time:	Date:
Name of person raising issue:	
Issue arising:	
Options or actions considered: 1. 2. 3. (continue as required)	
Decision made/ actions taken:	
Reasons for decision made/ actions taken:	
Name of incident management team Chair or Deputy: Signature of incident management team Chair or Deputy:	
Additional remarks:	

Note: this is an example which can be tailored to suit individual businesses.

Appendix 'B'

Model agenda for first meeting of incident management team

Using a model agenda is a good way to begin any series of incident management meetings. Circumstances may be different, but there are a few general principles which can be followed. Meetings should last no more than 25-30 minutes:-

1. Introduction and apologies.
2. Initial briefing on the situation by Chair or other individual involved.
3. Do the people there have the authority to make decisions and deploy resources without referral to a higher authority?
4. Rules for the conduct of meetings.
5. What are the implications for the businesses represented at the meeting?
6. What options have been considered and what are the recommendations for remediation, if any?
7. Agree items for action and allocate tasks – initiate focus board and situation reports.
8. Chair or Deputy to sum up actions and ensure those tasked understand what is required of them.
9. Fix the time of the next meeting.

Agenda for subsequent meetings

1. Introduction and apologies.
2. Review minutes and actions from previous meeting.
3. Situation update and feedback from other meetings which may have taken place.
4. Review outstanding issues from members.
5. Agree items for action and allocate tasks.
6. Shift hand-over arrangements if incident is likely to become protracted
7. Any other competent business.
8. Time of next meeting.

Flexibility is the key and businesses should tailor the examples to suit their own circumstances.

Appendix 'C'

Using focus boards

Maintaining a focus board is a good way to keep the attention of the incident management team on the immediate priorities which need to be addressed. A white board or flip chart can be used for the purpose, but it is important that it is kept refreshed with the priorities the incident management team deem the most vital.

Whilst there will be many things to occupy the attention of the team, there should be no more than 6 -7 items listed as headings on the focus board. On average the human brain can only hold about 7 pieces of information; therefore some hard choices may have to be made as to what the most vital priorities are for the team. Items which have been satisfactorily resolved should be removed from the list.

It is important that the incident management team does not try to take on too much, and concentrates on what is vitally important to the survival of the business. There will be tasks which are essential and there will be some which, although important in their own right, can be left during the emergency, even if it means more work to fix the problems later on.

Deciding what is vital will not be an easy task. Members of the incident management team will have to call on all their knowledge and experience to make hard and difficult decisions which will decide whether the business recovers or fails.

There may also be tensions in the team about what is and what is not vital, and these differences will have to be overcome if the team is to have any chance of recovering the business. Compromises *will* have to be reached.

Appendix 'D'

Appointment of a briefing officer and preparation of situation reports

A briefing officer should be appointed by the Chair of the incident management team. Situation reports should be prepared at regular intervals for the information of senior management and others involved in the management of the incident, who may not be part of the incident management team.

Reports should be posted on an information board so that new incident team members have knowledge of what has happened in addition to any briefing by the colleague they are relieving.

Reports should be clear and concise so that the information can be easily assimilated by the reader. They should be short, probably no longer than two A4 pages, and there are a few basic rules to follow when completing them:-

1. Reports to be sequentially numbered, dated and timed, and endorsed with the name of the author.
2. Begin with a short summary of what happened. The who, what, where, when, why, and how of what happened.
3. The content must be clear to the reader and the use of technical jargon, acronyms and abbreviations avoided. Use plain language writing styles.
4. The content must be concise. Don't make the input wordy. Say only what is necessary to convey the message.
5. The content must paint an accurate picture of what has taken place.
6. The report must contain current information that covers the last reporting period and should not repeat what was in the previous report unless there is some major relevance.
7. The report must deal with critical events and activities with detail on the status or completion of those events and activities.
8. Use facts and figures and avoid supposition and speculation.

Appendix 'E'

Message/action record form – incoming calls and messages

Incoming call		Message serial no:	
	Date:	Time:	
Call received by:			
Name of incoming caller:			
Tel. no. of incoming caller			
Location of incoming caller:			
Message for:			
Text of message:			
Action taken:			
Name of person handling call:	Signature:		
	Cross reference to other message no:		

Note: this is an example only and should be tailored to suit the needs of individual businesses.

Appendix 'E' (continued)
Message/action record form – outgoing calls and messages

Outgoing call		Message serial no:	
	Date:	Time:	
Call made by:			
Name of person receiving call:			
Tel. no. of person receiving call:			
Location of person receiving call:			
Message for:			
Text of message:			
Action taken:			
Signature:			
Cross reference to message no:			

Note: this is an example only and should be tailored to suit the needs of individual businesses.

Appendix 'F'

Debriefing the incident

It is essential that a formal de-brief of the incident is carried out to capture lessons identified by the incident management team members and others before it fades from memory.

Below is a format based on the National Decision Model produced by the Association of Chief Police Officers. It can be adapted to suit the requirements of individual businesses:-

Information

1. What information or intelligence was available?
2. Did the internal mechanism for calling the incident management team together work effectively?

Assessment

3. Which factors, such as hazards and potential benefits, were assessed?
4. What threat assessment methods were used, if any?
5. Was the strategy & tactics implemented to manage the incident appropriate?

Policy

6. Were there any company policies or regulatory legislation that should have been considered?
7. If company policy was not followed, was it reasonable in the circumstances?

Options

8. How were options for remediation identified and assessed?

Action and review

9. Were decisions proportionate, necessary and ethical?
10. Were decisions reasonable in the circumstances facing the incident management team?
11. Were decisions communicated effectively throughout the business and to customers, suppliers, regulators and others with an interest?

12. Were decisions and the rationale for them recorded as appropriate?
13. Were decisions monitored and reassessed where necessary?
14. What lessons can be taken from the outcomes and how the decisions were made?

For senior managers
15. Were instances of initiative or good decisions acknowledged, and were they passed to managers where appropriate?
16. Were instances of poor decision making recognised and challenged?
17. In instances where the outcome was not what was hoped for, if the decision taken by staff was reasonable given the circumstances, they still deserve support. Remember mistakes will be made!

Appendix 'G'

Action plan following a live event or emergency exercise.

The action plan should ideally be in table form to suit the individual business unit, and include the following information:-

1. Serial number of the action;

2. Description of the learning point, including the name of the group or individual that identified it;

3. The action required to address the learning point;

4. The 'owner' or named person assigned to complete the action;

5. The projected date for completion of the action;

6. The progress of the action along with any reasons for a delay;

7. The date the action plan was reviewed by the Chair of the incident management team or other reviewing officer;

8. Any remarks or comments made by the reviewing officer;

9. The name and signature of the reviewing officer.

References

1. The National Decision Model – (Association of Chief Police Officers, England & Wales)

2. Cambridge Dictionaries Online (http://dictionary.cambridge.org/)

3. Federation of Small Businesses (http://www.fsb.org.uk/eastanglia/business-continuity)

4. Good Practice Guidelines, (Business Continuity Institute), 2013 (http://thebci.org/).

5. Jonathan Hemus, (Insignia Reputation Management & Communications Consultancy), (Continuity Central, January, 2009) (http://continuitycentral.com/feature0638.html).

6. 'STAC' Guidance – Scottish Government, 2008 (http://www.scotland.gov.uk/Publications/2013/02/6297/0)

7. UK Government Cabinet Office, (https://www.gov.uk/government/publications/business-continuity-guide-sample-chapter--2)

www.ingramcontent.com/pod-product-compliance
Lightning Source LLC
Chambersburg PA
CBHW051823170526
45167CB00005B/2130